MW01240621

*1*

# The Concrete Muse

*A Manny Flores Memoir.*

# Letter from the Author:

*I began this book at the age of 22. Not knowing what kind of life is in store for me, I ask that you take this journey along with me. They tried leaving me for dead, but they didn't realize that I was a survivor. I dedicate this book to my mother, Flor Hernandez - thank you for all your courage and wisdom. I hope to leave a mark in this world that will last forever. I want to give a huge shoutout to Jermaine Cole - you gave people like me a voice. To all the young kids everywhere, no dream or obstacle is too big, so keep on believing.*

*-Manny Flores*

# *Preface:*

My name is Manny Flores, and this is my story, told through my eyes, and about my experiences. I wasn't sure if this was the right thing to do, to publish my book, being that it is so early in my career, and I have so much more living to do. I told myself that if I did publish this book, I would want it to mean something ten years from now. I want people to read my story and be so inspired afterwards that they challenge themselves to be better people. I came to this country illegally, had to learn a new language, was in and out of probation, but most importantly, I successfully navigated my way through a system that was designed to oppress students of color. By no means was anything handed to me - please use my story to fuel your fire and to assure you that if you work hard towards something, you can achieve it. I have worked extremely hard over the last couple of years, so I'm excited to share this piece of myself and open up to you all. Never in a million years did I think I would be publishing a book about my life, but I think this will help a lot of people find themselves. I hope that at the end of this journey, you try to find your purpose in life, because we all have one.

If you find yourself at a low point when you are reading this, know that nothing is ever constant. You can't control the fire around you, but you can control the fire in your head. Just work on yourself every day, and good things will happen, I promise. I found myself at rock bottom and forced myself to get better. I was never alone though -- I used the only positive thing around me, which was my relationship with my mother, and together, we went to community college and enrolled myself into school.There were times where I wanted to give up, but my mother didn't allow me to quit on myself. As of now, I am a couple of months away from applying to Harvard, for my Phd in Education. I am currently 23 years old, with the whole world ahead of me. I'm currently still undocumented, hoping that things get better one day. Whoever is reading this, just know that you matter, and that your story needs to be heard. Also, remember this - the only person that can stop you from achieving greatness is yourself, so get what's yours. I'm not going to lie, it's a struggle at times, and a process, but part of growing means opening yourself up, and even being vulnerable at times. Know that this is a part of the grind and it comes with life. Anything in life is achievable, ya dig?

# Table Of Contents:

## *Letter to My 16 Year-Old Self:*

Dear Manny,

It is okay to cry and to not be sure about what your place in this world is. Everything you are doing right now has a purpose, even the bad. Just continue to better yourself and never stop asking questions. You are curious as to how the world works, and believe me, those curiosities will manifest themselves into something great. All I can tell you is, hard times don't last, so just keep fighting. You have the skills, and just because people can't see them right now, it doesn't mean you aren't valuable. You will go far in life, just continue putting God first and appreciating the good people around you. Don't stress about your friends or drama, most of that stuff won't matter in a couple of years anyway.

Can you see yourself being a doctor one day?
Well guess what, that's going to happen. What if
I told you that in a few years, you will be
applying for your Phd? You hold the keys to
your future - just stop getting in trouble. Mom
cares about you, stop treating her bad and taking
advantage of the fact that she's never home.
Things are going to get hard before they get
better. You will hit rock bottom and feel lower
than you ever felt before- that's okay though, it's
part of the growth. Pressure makes diamonds,
and after you propel yourself from the pitfalls,
you will see everything get better.


-Manny Flores

November 21, 2017 (24 years old)

# 1
## Humble Beginnings

*"I never did anything I'm really ashamed of."*                   *—Lauryn Hill*

My story begins in another country. I was
born on October 13, 1993, in Acapulco, Mexico.
I only remember a few things from my time in
Mexico - almost drowning in a river, meeting
my father in prison for the first time, and the day
I crossed the border and arrived in the United
States. I am the youngest of four siblings, and

*14*

from what I can remember, life in Mexico was a lot of fun. That was the only time I ever remember feeling like I had a complete family - I had uncles, aunties, and even my grandmother. My mom had five brothers and sisters, so I always had a lot of cousins to play with. At the time, I was too young to understand, but my mom had dreams of us coming to the United States because life in Mexico was very difficult. My mom would oftentimes work a full day of work and receive very little pay afterwards. She always had a vision that we would have better lives one day, and not have to struggle among poverty and violence.

Where I lived was very dangerous -- often times, people were robbed for their money and belongings, regardless of their age. My mom shared stories with me about my grandma going out for groceries and being mugged for everything she had. For Christmas, my mom bought her some gold earrings, and the robbers ended up pulling them out of her ears while she was on the way to pick us up from school. While I was in Mexico, I attended a private school that offered a lot of different programs, such as English and swimming classes. When the school year was coming to an end, they had informed my mom that I would have to retake the first grade, because I wasn't old enough to be in the second grade. My mom got really upset, because the school had charged us for a whole year's worth of tuition, and they weren't planning on giving us a refund. My mom wanted to give me and my sister, Lily, a better education, and she figured we would get that in the United States of America. My mom decided to pack up her stuff and left for the United States by herself--with nothing. She essentially was sacrificing herself, as there was no assurance that she would make it to the United States alive - she had to cross the border by foot.

I was only four years old when my mother left, and I couldn't comprehend why she was gone. My mom figured that it was best if my sister and I stayed behind while she found a place for us to live in the United States and saved enough money to be able to support us. It would be a whole year before we would see her again, as she left my sister and I at our grandmother's house. During that year, my grandma took care of us - she would walk me to and pick me up from school every morning.

I grew up without my dad - the saddest part about it was that he named me after himself, only to leave my mom and me to deal with this world by ourselves. When my mother was pregnant with me, my parents divorced, and he moved away with another family. My dad was apparently doing some shady stuff, as he ended up going to jail for kidnapping a man, and got sentenced to 10 years in a federal Mexican prison. When my father found out that my mom was leaving for the United States, he wanted to see my sister one last time, and to meet me for the first time. I think it's crazy that I was four years old and meeting him for the first time, but

I remember very vividly how that day went.

I remember meeting this tall, dark man in a brown khaki jumpsuit. I specifically remember him buying me chocolate cookies, the ones that come in an eight pack. That would be the first, and last time, that I would see my father. Me and my sister left and went back to my grandmother's house. My mother eventually called and told us that she had made it past the border and into the United States. To this very day, I commend that woman for being strong enough to go through the rigorous desert that separates Mexico and the United States. My mom had some extended family living in the San Francisco Bay Area, so she made her way over there and quickly began working to save enough money to be able to bring my sister and me across the border. My mom's first job was working at an ice cream shop - she was determined to do whatever it took to see her kids again. After a year passed, my mom had enough money saved up, and she started the process of bringing us to America. At the time, my oldest brother, Raul (24), had a kid and a wife, so he wasn't able to drop everything and move with us and had to stay in Mexico. To this day, I haven't seen him since the day I left for the United States.

My oldest sister, Flor (18), was going to a prestigious university in Mexico, so she couldn't move with us either. My sister went on to graduate as a medical doctor. I was 6 at the time, and my other sister, Lily, was 12, so we were the only ones that moved to the United States. I remember very vividly as we flew in an airplane to Tijuana from Acapulco, where we met some relatives that would help bring us into the country. My mother had cousins that lived in San Diego, CA, and would frequently travel back and forth to Mexico.

That morning, they drove to the airport in Tijuana to pick up me and my sister. They were going to drive us across the border, to their house, which was in San Diego. We crossed the border in a car, and they told me to act like I was sleeping so that they wouldn't ask me any questions. When it was our turn to get our car inspected, I closed my eyes and acted like I was asleep. They checked the driver's papers and just like that, we crossed the border. I was finally in the United States, where I would spend the rest of my life. After a whole day of traveling, I ended up arriving in San Leandro, California, and reuniting with my mother and sister. My mom had a small, two bedroom house that she had rented, with the help of my uncle, on Cascade Rd.

## 2
### Cascade Rd.

*"To appreciate the sun, you gotta know what rain is"*    *- J. Cole*

The first day I showed up to San Leandro, my mom greeted me with a Pokemon shirt and a Pokemon book - I was only six at the time. San Leandro is a small city on the outskirts of Oakland, California. Our house was a very old and small home, with two bedrooms and one bathroom. However, it was perfect for us, just perfect. The street I lived on was called Cascade Rd. Although it was my mother, sister, uncle and I living in the same house, we made it work. I came to the United States in the month of August, just in time to begin school. I was placed in the second grade, but because I didn't know any English, I got put in bilingual classes. I guess I have always been naturally good at making friends, because I talk a lot. Due to some cultural differences, it took me awhile to get used to living here. Just the language barrier alone made it hard to understand things, so I was always lost. I remember wanting to play soccer all the time, while the other kids wanted to play football instead. My mother would do her best to try and keep me sheltered while I was growing up, but trouble follows everyone, no matter how much you avoid it.

One day while in school, me and my friend, Daniel, thought it would be funny to throw a girl in the boy's bathroom, so we did. We pushed her in the bathroom and didn't let her out. The funny part about it was that she had a crush on Daniel, so she went and told on us, but said it was only me. I got in trouble and my mom was forced to buy her a new backpack because we ripped hers. In elementary school, I would have a hard time staying quiet and focused. I was diagnosed with ADHD early on, but my mother didn't want me to be on medication, so I had to try my best to control it. I always had a lot of energy, so people assumed that I was a bad kid who liked getting in trouble, but the reality was, I couldn't sit still. Life in the classroom, as opposed to my neighborhood, was very different. Some of the kids in the neighborhood would only speak English, so we couldn't communicate with one another, but as kids, we kinda understood what the other was saying. My English eventually started to get better as I progressed further in elementary school. Often times, my mother would struggle to make ends meet - sometimes, she would work 12 hour shifts and still have to come home and cook.

I remember my mom being scared to leave me and my sister at home by ourselves because she didn't want Child Protective Services to take us away. Instead, she would bring us to her job and leave us in the car while she was at work. I would be in my mom's car for up to five hours sometimes, and I remember doing my homework while I would wait. There used to be a McDonald's next to her job, so she would buy me happy meals, and the toys would keep me entertained. Because we were undocumented, we lived life in the shadows, always worried that we would be deported if we did not follow the rules. I grew up always feeling confused, because I never felt like I belonged or knew what my place was. I understood that I wasn't American, but was learning more and more about the history of the country while also forgetting my own.

Having ADHD and not understanding English made it hard to focus in class. I would act out a lot, causing me to always get sent out of the room. Things at home weren't going well either. The relationship between me and Lily was pretty bad at the time. Lily was six years older than me, and sometimes, she would take out her frustrations on me. Witnessing my parent's divorce must have taken a toll on her, and it affected her really badly. Often times, Lily would beat me unconscious and leave me there, crying and beaten. I remember one time, she called my friends to come watch me get beat up, almost like an exhibition. I was on the ground crying, while my friends and sister laughed at me. The worst part about that experience is that an hour later, something would make Lily realize how cruel she was treating me, so she would come to me crying, asking for my forgiveness. I would sit there, in so much pain, and she would come sit next to me, hug me, and cry with me, but the disturbing part is, I always forgave her--every time. I think that influenced how I treated people, because no matter what she did to me, and how much pain she caused me, I always had to forgive her.

I started noticing this pattern when I started hurting people and expecting them to just forgive me. When I was younger, I used to be scared of the dark, so my sister would tease me. She would threaten me by turning the lights off and leaving me in the room by myself. One day, she was teasing me and almost turned the lights off. I got scared, so I ran to try to beat her out of the room. I ended up tripping and fell head first into the stairs. I fractured a bone in my face and required 15 stitches. To this day, I have a big scar across my eyebrow - thanks, Lily.

## 3
### Innocent Bystander

"When you reach the end of your rope, tie a knot in it and hang on."
                              -Franklin D. Roosevelt

I eventually graduated elementary school. My
English was getting better, and my view of the
world was changing. Going to junior high was a
big change for me, as I was starting to become a
young adult. At that time, my mom was still
picking out and buying my clothes, and would

even choose the haircut I could get. Although some of my classmates were wearing Jordans and other cool stuff, I was forced to wear off-brand clothes, like Yu-gi-oh shirts, and other clothing that was out of style. By no means was I the cool kid, or anything like it - in fact, I was the complete opposite. I would hear the word "paisa" a lot, and that's basically saying that I looked like someone that came straight out of Mexico. I remember being so innocent and not knowing how the world worked. There were kids in the 6th grade that were already dating and having sex. I didn't even have the courage to talk to girls yet, so it was crazy to me to see kids growing up so fast. I spent most of my middle school years observing and thinking about what it was like to talk to girls and wear cool clothes.

One day, I was feeling the pressure, because all my friends were having sex already, and being a virgin was embarrassing. One day, I walked up to a girl I liked and asked her to be my girlfriend - she said no and left me crushed.

That day was one of the saddest days in my life - I got flat out rejected, and I didn't like how that felt. Growing up, I was never an aggressive kid. I would get in trouble, but it would be for disrupting the class, as opposed to harmful behavior, like fighting. My first fight came in middle school, however - I fought this kid named Justin, who also lived in my neighborhood. My sister was there, and she wouldn't let me stop fighting unless I won. I specifically remember wanting to stop fighting, but I had to continue getting up and coming for more. All I could hear my sister say was "Manny, you better not stop, keep going." I think I fought for like ten minutes.

I finally got my first girlfriend in middle school, but it didn't last long, maybe like two weeks, tops. Some kids in my middle school were really bad -- I remember there were kids who were drinking and smoking, and even stealing cars. There were these kids that would tell me stories of how they would do ecstasy and steal a bunch of stuff. All I could do was watch and listen, because I didn't have anything to share or add to the story. Those same stories turned into juvenile hall stories and again, all I could do was listen. The kids in my neighborhood started a gang, and they asked me to join. In order for me to be allowed in, I had to get "jumped in" in order to be a member. I remember having to fight my friend for a few seconds, and after that was done, I was an official member. At the time, not having a father crucially impacted my development - at any point, he could've talked to me and stopped me from looking up to those negative things and eventually, wanting to imitate my friends. If my father had been involved at the time, to answer all those questions about what I was going through, I don't think I would have turned out the way that I did.

My first sexual experience with a girl happened in the 8th grade. I remember crushing on her, so we would pass notes back and forth.

We eventually made it over to her house, where we would kiss, but I didn't know how to take it any further. I was shy and didn't know what I was doing. I remember wanting to take it further - I just didn't want to be a virgin anymore, but I struck out. During 8th grade was also the first time I tried smoking weed, but I wasn't successful at it. I remember that no one knew how to roll a blunt, so we did a horrible job and tried smoking it, but we couldn't. At the time, I had not been introduced to weed, so I was surprised that some of my classmates already knew what it was and had tried it. Another big factor in my school was the gang influence. It felt like it was the army, the way they were trying to recruit everyone to join. I felt like by the time kids got to high school, they had to pick what gang they wanted to be a part of, and everyone had to chose. I remember some of my friends couldn't walk the stage for our 8th grade graduation because of their gang affiliations. After the 8th grade, I lost all of my innocence.

*4*

*Ken Griffey Jr.*

"There is nothing permanent except
change." -Heraclitus

I started 9th grade feeling pretty lost and still
didn't know how the world worked. The first day
of school, I remember wearing an all red shirt -
at the time, it probably wasn't a good idea
because of all the gang influence that was going
on at that moment. Red was a color used by one

of the gangs at my school. Within five minutes of being there, I got approached by someone who started asking me a bunch of questions. I started high school when I was 13 years old, as a freshman - the person that approached me was like 17, so he was older and bigger than me. He asked me if I was Lily's little brother, to which I then replied "Yeah." He ended up telling me that he was good friends with her and that if I needed anything, don't hesitate to let him know. I was so relieved that someone wasn't trying to fight me, so I proceeded on with my day. In 9th grade, my English was pretty good, and I was starting to mix in with the culture. This was the first year my mom let me pick out my own clothes, so I was able to dress like my peers, which was very important to me. For the first time, I was going to fit in with my other classmates, thus giving me a sense of belonging.

Since my school was next to Oakland, we had a lot of kids transfer in from there, and at the time, the Bay Area's crime rate was very high, causing everyone to always be on full alert. I generally tried to stay out of trouble, for the most part, because I didn't want to jeopardize my chances of making the baseball team. At this time, baseball was the only positive thing I had going for me. I tried out for the team, and it took a few weeks to determine who was going to stay and who was going to get cut. Originally, I made the 12 man roster, but when they found out I had under a 2.0 GPA, I was cut from the baseball team. At that time, baseball was all I thought about - I was still trying to be a Major League Baseball player at the time, and I didn't have a plan B. I naturally stopped hanging out with the baseball players once I got cut and began finding another identity. I eventually started smoking heavily in the 9th grade, before and after school, and I noticed my life taking a turn for the worse.

I popped ecstasy for the first time in the 9th grade as well. I guess I was eager to try it because of all those stories I would hear in middle school about my friends doing it. I always knew that if I had a chance, I would do similar things, because I looked up to my friends. My experience was very trippy - I remember being in class when the pill started to kick in. I began feeling like I had immediately grown eight feet, and I was suddenly this giant kid in the classroom, but everyone else was still their regular size. I was in another world, and the crazy part was that I was in class. The class eventually ended, and I left to go tell my friends about my experience. I remember thinking to myself that I would pop another pill again, because I loved how it was making me feel.

Being from the Bay Area and being Latino, people often made it seem like we had to join a gang or pick a side, because if you were cool with both sides, that meant you were fake. In my neighborhood, there was a gang that was very popular, so in a way, the choice had been made for me since the first day I moved into that neighborhood. I think the pressure of trying to fit in and seeming cool made me do things that I didn't want to do. Graffiti was very big at the time as well, so I would buy spray paint and go tag buildings up. One time, I had a big marker, so I tagged up my classroom. I ended up getting in trouble with my teacher, and security had to come and escort me to the principal's office. At the time, I had about three spray paint cans in my backpack, because me and my friend had plans to meet up after school and paint. I ended up getting suspended for five days, and my mom had to come pick me up from school. My mom started work at 2 p.m. and wouldn't get off until midnight, making it impossible for her to ground me or punish me. I think that made me even worse - the fact that I knew I would never get in trouble, no matter what I did, because no one would be home. I continued in my ways, and nothing ever got better.

Eventually, I got so mad that I wouldn't even care what my own mother said, and I would completely blow her off. I was starting to be very defiant and not really care about the consequences. At the time, my mom and I would get into a lot of verbal disputes, and when she felt like she couldn't control me, she would try to put her hands on me, and we eventually started fighting.

Fighting with my mom never felt good -- in fact, it made me feel worse. I knew she couldn't tell me what to do anymore. The fights were nothing more than her trying to hit me and me defending myself. My uncle was the only male figure in my life, but he failed to be there for me. I can now realize that I would have never taken his advice -- after all, "he wasn't my dad." That's what I would tell him whenever he tried telling me anything.

# 5

## Mr. Dixon

"My moms always told me, 'How long you gonna play the victim?' I can say I'm mad and I hate everything, but nothing really changes until I change myself."
            -Kendrick Lamar

When I started my sophomore year, I was a whole new person. I felt like I was getting out of control. I was one year removed from sports, which meant I no longer had any positive influences in my life. At this point, doing bad and trying to live the street life was embedded in me. Because I was never good at school to begin with, it made it easier to drop out and not really focus on my schoolwork - after all, "school isn't for everyone," so that was my excuse. I noticed a trend starting to happen with my demeanor, and how my clothes started changing - I was starting to become a new person. At this time in my life, I was 14 years old, and I was just looking up to everything and everyone because I didn't have anything of my own. I had a girlfriend at the time, and even her own mom was selling drugs and into the same kind of lifestyle I looked up to. One night, I was at their house and the police broke into the house, because they had a warrant to raid the property. Me and my ex-girlfriend got put in handcuffs and were put in the living room as they continued checking the house for drugs -- I was only 15. My girlfriend's mom was married to a woman and, during the raid, they found a kilo of crystal meth in her possession and deported her the same night. Nights like that showed me a valuable lesson - everything can be over so quickly: your life, your love, and your family. Because my mom didn't know any English and did not necessarily understand the culture, it made me feel like I did not belong either, so that made me not care. My life was on a downward spiral, and no one could stop me from spinning out of control.

At the time, I had a teacher named Mr. Dixon. He was a heavier guy, very loud, but he cared for all of his students. He was one of the few teachers you could feel actually cared and wasn't there just to collect a paycheck. At times, he would treat you like a son, and that made me feel good. If he would see a student walking around in the hallway, he would stop you and make you return to class. Mr. Dixon would often use examples from his own life to try to teach us a lesson. He would talk to us about his family and would tell us stories from high school. If at any moment he caught you talking to a classmate or not paying attention, he would make you go outside and run. Mr. Dixon would sometimes make the entire class run if the class got bad test scores, or if no one could answer his math questions. One time, I remember that he tried to fight me - while the class was in session, he closed the door and squared up to me in front of the whole class. This man was at least 200 pounds bigger than me, so I had to just stand there like a punk, because I knew he would have whooped me.

Besides Mr. Dixon, I never felt like any adult wanted me to succeed, or even cared to try to help. During my sophomore year in high school, I was failing all my classes (mostly because of cutting). In fact, I received a 0.17 GPA, and my life was heading towards disaster. With my mom never being home and no father to punish me, I was completely out of control. I could get suspended at school for five days and no one would be at home to say anything to me. During my sophomore year, I would spend most of my time with my then-girlfriend - her parents would be okay with me spending the night and coming over all the time. We would be allowed to smoke weed all the time and basically do anything we wanted. One of her mom's friends would come over all the time as well. Nick had recently been in a motorcycle accident, so he would be on a lot of pain killers. Nick was a middle aged white guy that was in love with my ex-girlfriend's mom. He would do anything to be on her good side-- he would take us out to dinner and sometimes, even the movies. Nick believed that if he was in good standing with us, then my ex's mom would want to be with him. We would take advantage of this and make him give us money. Eventually, we convinced him to give us some of his pain killers -- we would take like four at a time. I was 15 years old, experimenting with different prescription drugs. One time, Nick passed out while driving, so I had to drive his truck while I was intoxicated myself. I ended up coming home around 12 a.m., and my mom was mad at the fact that I came home so late and looked like I was on a lot of drugs. My mom slapped me, and out of instinct, I pushed her and tried to hold her down.

We started fighting at that point, and I guess we were being loud enough that the neighbors called the police. The police came to my door and took me to the police station. I got booked into juvenile hall that night for assault and battery charges - I was only 15. All the stories my friends started telling me about juvenile hall suddenly started popping up in my head. I quickly remembered all the advice they shared with me. They told me to walk in there like I had just killed someone, and to not be intimidated by anyone in there, so I did just that. I remember walking into juvenile hall, with all the kids looking through their glass doors at the new kid coming in. I was also looking at every single kid in the eyes, letting them know I wasn't a punk. I quickly realized that I was going to be miserable in that place. The 30-unit cell was cold, and the

*43*

smell made you want to throw up. For lunch and dinner, we got soggy food and a carton of milk. I spent the weekend in juvenile hall and got released on Monday. All the stories I heard were true, but most importantly in my mind, I got validation for finally reaching a milestone - getting locked up. My mother didn't press charges, so I was released without having to go to court. I went home and continued on my road to destruction.

# 6
## *Thizzle Dance*

*"It is better to die on your feet than to live on your knees." -Emiliano Zapata*

Junior year was by far my favorite year of my high school career. I felt like I was really starting to come into my own, in terms of my personality and style. I had been in high school for enough time to really understand who I was and what I wanted to be-- or so I thought. At this point, I was selling drugs and consistently doing them. I felt like I was popular for all the wrong things. I naturally got along with all the seniors and all the underclassmen, which made it easier to have friends. By no means was I thinking about life after high school or college - after all, people like me didn't attend college. I kept moving forward on my path of destruction.

My high school offered trade courses, such as construction or collision repair. I joined the constructuction department and was hoping to find my niche, but I was quickly kicked out because of poor behavior. I felt like no matter what I was touching, it was constantly breaking. I found myself, at 16, failing in school, failing at home, and most importantly, failing in life. My neighbor at the time, Carlos, loved to steal cars, so he showed me how to break into them. Halfway through junior year, I had stolen close to 30 cars and had never gotten caught. Whenever I would break into cars, I would make sure all the lights worked, so that I had no reason to get pulled over by the cops.

One night, we were in Oakland, getting gas. As soon as we turned out of the gas station, a cop pulled us over -- we had no plans on stopping. I got into my first high speed chase with the police. I remember going 70 mph in a 25 mph zone and being scared for my life. We noticed the street was coming to an end, so we pressed the brakes fast and the car lost control. We crashed into a wall and got out of the car. Afterwards, we started running towards the train tracks. I reached a barbed wire fence - at this point, my freedom was the first thing on my mind. I took my jacket off and tried to block the fence as best as I could. I jumped the fence and part of my pants got caught onto it. When I jumped down, my pants got ripped, but I kept going. I eventually made it to a Mcdonald's that was open. I called my girlfriend to come pick me up. Her and her mom came and picked me up and just like that, I got away from a high speed chase. I didn't know what happened to Carlos or anyone else that was in the car that night.

The next day, I came to school like nothing had happened. Instead of receiving counseling for that traumatic experience, I got thrown in the classroom and forced to learn about algebra. Later that day, I found out that Carlos had gotten caught and was at juvenile hall. Carlos ended up doing about three weeks in juvenile hall and got released on probation. The day he got out, we continued popping ecstasy pills and breaking into cars. One night, me and Carlos needed a car, so we stole a Honda. I quickly noticed that the front headlights were out, so I knew to get another car. My friend convinced me that we would be okay for the time being and that we would get another car before the night was over. I should have listened to my intuition, because five minutes later, a cop got behind us and turned on his sirens. We had no choice but to get into another high speed chase - after all, it was do or die.

We took them through back roads, trying to shake them off, but it just wasn't working. I remember being scared, but I couldn't show it. We finally got out of the car and started running and jumping fences--again. I remember the adrenaline running through my body and feeling a big rush. I was running and jumping as hard as I could. I eventually took cover in someone's backyard until the coast was clear. I could hear the dogs barking and the helicopter over me - it was like a scene in a movie.

I waited in the backyard for about an hour, and then I proceeded to go home. I jumped the fence, which was going to leave me on the street, when I heard "Get on the ground now." I took a look to my left and there was a cop moving in my direction, running full speed with his gun pointed at me. I laid on the ground and he proceeded to arrest me -- I had class the next day. While I was getting booked at the police station, I was being very disrespectful, calling the officers names and being loud. The part that made me sad is how much I was hurting my mom in the process. They called my mom at

3:00 a.m. to let her know that I was being arrested and booked into juvenile hall. My mom was on the phone with the cops, telling them that they had the wrong kid, because her son was in the bedroom, sleeping. When my mom went to my room and realized I wasn't in there, it broke her heart.

I got booked into juvenile hall just a few hours later. I realized I was becoming institutionalized, as I already knew how the process went. They would make me take off my street clothes, along with any jewelry, and put it in a bag. They gave me my light blue t-shirt, a blue crew neck, along with my khaki pants, and my velcro strap-on shoes. Juvenile hall is an interesting place. Every kid is in there trying to prove that they are the alpha male. Everyone would constantly try to intimidate me to prove they were tougher than me. I would stay in my cell for most of the day. The only times I was allowed to come out were to eat, exercise, or take a shower. They offered classes and a chance for kids to receive units towards their diplomas. The classes were poorly ran, as most of the students were always disrupting the class. Juvenile hall was a jail, and it made everyone feel like an animal. I did my time and got released on 18 months probation, as well as placed on home supervision. I was ordered to stay at home, unless I was going to school or court, and I was subjected to random house visits. I was on the straight and narrow for about a week, and then I started going back to my old ways. I left for a friend's house on Friday night and started drinking. I eventually got so drunk that I wasn't able to go home, so I stayed the night at my friend's place. My probation officer went to my house the following morning and I wasn't there; I had violated my probation. Ms. Felix was a very nice lady, but she was a no-nonsense type of woman. She called me and my mom in for a meeting. I learned quickly that I wasn't going to be leaving. I got detained that day for violating my probation, so I had to go back into juvenile hall. That feeling was like no other, getting taken against your will and not being able to do anything about it.

I had to go back to the khakis and to spending 14 hours a day alone in my cell. While I would be locked away in my room, I would talk to God and pray every day. I knew I didn't want to be bad, but there wasn't any other option for me to turn to. I eventually got released on probation, only this time with an ankle monitor, and had a few more months of supervision added to my sentence. I didn't want to continue to keep going to jail, so I tried to change my ways. I was constantly getting drug tested, so I stopped smoking weed completely, but quickly picked up alcohol instead. The liquor store by my house would sell me alcohol at 16 years old, so it made it really easy for me to get it. Me and my friends would drink two 4Lokos every day and would get really drunk. I would go to school with a hangover and would have to leave class sometimes so that I could go throw up. I was the devil's partner in crime, and I couldn't stop myself. I feel like trouble followed me everywhere I went. One day, I was on my way to the liquor store, but in order for me to get there, I had to go through the creek, which was behind people's homes. While I was standing next to someone's home by the creek, a man came out of his house and confronted me as to why I was in his backyard.

He had a shotgun pointed at me. I was so scared for my life that I honestly felt like that man was going to kill me right there, where I was standing. He asked me if I belonged in a gang and I told him "No." He told me that the rival gang spray painted his house a couple of days before that. We started talking and found out we had a lot of mutual friends, so he let me keep walking. That day, I looked at death in the face and realized how quickly I could've lost everything. Once again, I was determined to get back into being positive and staying out of trouble. Everyone in my school wanted to dress nice, and material items were starting to become very popular. My mom was never able to afford those things, so if I wanted them for myself, I would have to take measures into my own hands. Me and my friends started robbing people on the street every night. I was living in a fashion that no high school student should ever live. We would ride around in Oakland, looking for people to rob.

Whenever we would see anyone on the street walking, we would get out of the car and rob them with our gun. We would do this every night, but would only have a few dollars once we split it up equally. I managed to not get caught and eventually got off on probation. The school year was coming to an end, so it was time to celebrate. I decided to go to prom that year, so I went and got fitted for a tuxedo. The day of prom, I decided to pop three ecstasy pills -- some green apples. My junior year was a complete rollercoaster, from start to finish.

# 7
## 2500 Fairmont Drive

*"Freedom is never voluntarily given by the oppressor; it must be demanded by the oppressed." —Martin Luther King, Jr.*

I started senior year on more of a positive note, because I realized that I was almost out of high school, so I needed to start thinking about my future. A couple of weeks into school, I learned that I wasn't going to be able to graduate at the end of the year. I was missing too many credits and didn't have enough time to make them up. At that point, it was hard to remain positive when you know there is no prize at the end of the race, but I had no choice - I couldn't let the school system wear me down. I tried my best to get my work done, but it was hard to remain motivated under the weight of all of my history. Most of my friends had graduated the previous year, so I started to hang out by myself during school and at lunch. I was already thinking about life after high school and what that meant for me going forward. I knew that in my mind, I didn't want to be a drop out and not be able to provide for my future family. I started doing well in school and getting good grades. That senior year, I passed all my classes and started changing inside. I felt that I started changing in the sense that I no longer wanted to be completely negative and have people thinking I was a failure. The school year was coming to an end and I was on my grind. I was attending class regularly and trying to be positive. I went to prom that year -- despite knowing that I wasn't going to graduate, I wanted to feel like a senior and do senior activities.

Two weeks before school ended, I found out that a kid was selling weed at school, but he was a sucker - I knew I could take all his weed, so that's exactly what I did. Me and my friends set him up and robbed him for all his weed. At the time, one of my favorite rap groups rapped about committing crimes "bare faced," meaning without a mask, so I wanted to do the same. I committed the robbery without a mask while my two friends had theirs on. When we robbed him, he put up a light fight, but it was easy and we got away cleanly. For the next couple of days, we continued smoking and plotting on our next move.

One morning, I woke up to someone knocking on my door. I got out of bed, in my boxers, and went to open the door: it was the police. They said, "Manny Flores, you are being placed under arrest for robbery." They allowed me to put shorts and a shirt on and took me to the police station. Since it was two weeks after the robbery, I had forgotten that I had committed that particular crime. While I was in the station, I wasn't sure what was going to happen to me, or where my future was heading. The police kept asking me about the people I committed the crime with and insisting that if I named them, I could get a lesser sentence. Of course, I wasn't going to snitch - that was the first rule you learn growing up in the hood--snitches get stitches. I kept my mouth shut and waited until they sent me to juvenile hall.

Things felt different this time, due to the nature of how violent the crime was. The cops were treating me more harshly than before, and I just knew I was going to get punished severely for this one. I was institutionalized already, so I knew the drill, change into your khakis and baby blue t-shirt. The food was the worst part about the experience - they served you a hot and cold plate, and you'd be lucky to get a soggy cookie as a dessert. There were times that I would just give my food to someone because of how nasty it looked. Juvenile hall was a place where people didn't go to get better - in fact, it was the complete opposite. You were in a place that hosted 30 juveniles who were all competing to reach the top of the food chain. I waited for a couple of days to receive updates from the court hearing. During the initial hearing, I found out that they wanted to drop the hammer on me and make an example out of me. At the time, I was two months removed from turning 18, so they wanted to see if they could try me as an adult, or even possibly deport me. My future was no longer in my hands and I realized that, if these people wanted to, they could wash me away for good. While in jail, all I could do was be positive and try to think about ways I could improve my life. I was only allowed a few hours a day to come out of my cell -- to eat, shower, and stretch. The four walls that made up my cell became my friends, as I would talk to them daily. The cell was small, with only a sink, toilet, and a small bed. Every night I was in there, I would pray to God that he would look after me. I realized I had hit rock bottom - while my friends were walking the stage and graduating high school, I was in jail with no high school diploma. I realized that if I kept this up, I was going to end up going to jail for the rest of my life. That's when the horns blew - "Manny Flores, transfer."

The correctional officer came to my room to tell me that I was being transferred to the max security unit. I didn't know what max security meant - he told me that it is where all the most violent criminal offenders go, and that I would not be allowed contact visits. A non-contact visit is when you are forced to talk to your visitor behind the glass screen with the phone. While walking in max security, everyone was staring at me, trying to figure out what I was about. But these weren't amateur criminals, these were people who were already convicted of murder.

The state was waiting for them to turn 18 so that they could send them to prison.

After a few minor confrontations, I was settled in to what was to be my new home. I noticed that one of my classmates was in the same unit as me, so I quickly joined up with him. There was someone else I ran into while in max security that I knew - we had kicked it in Oakland once before. I told him about that time, and he remembered me also. I asked him what he was in there for, and he told me he had murdered someone and had gotten sentenced to 25 years to life at age 17. Being that my case was still pending, I was scared that I was going to get an extreme sentence, so I started freaking out in my cell. I would pray and pray and ask God to please let me get out so that I could change my life for good. I had hit rock bottom.

Waking up every day and not having any certainty about your future or where you were going to end up was driving me crazy. There were days that I would fall asleep crying because

I was so scared. One day, I woke up and made a promise to myself to never end up in another jail cell. I realized that this wasn't how I wanted to live my life. I kept going to court, as the trial was ongoing. I would try and beg the judge to consider trying me as a juvenile, so that I could continue with my education. Apparently, she saw something in me, because she would go on to try me as a youth and not give me an adult sentence. The final court verdict came and I had a deal on the table. The deal was to plead guilty, receive a strike on my record, and be allowed to get released on house arrest and 18 months probation. That day, my prayers were answered. I was going to be allowed to get a second chance and get released from juvenile hall. I left my unit that day and headed straight to the probation department, where I got my ankle monitor put on, and the terms of my probation were explained to me.

I was to remain home at all times, unless I had permission from my probation officer to leave. When I got out, there were a few weeks left of summer, but I was determined to never go back to jail ever again. The same day I got released, my mom took me to an independent studies continuation school, where I was going to be allowed to finish up my remaining credits and receive my high school diploma. That summer, I was given seven packets, which were going to allow me to make up 35 units out of the 50 that I needed. That summer, I stayed busy and completed every single packet. I was constantly getting drug tested, so I was forced to get clean and not do any drugs. That summer came to an end, and I had completed every packet for school and tested clean for every drug. I enrolled into community college that fall after I told my mother that I wanted to see if I had what it took. We arrived at College of Alameda, and I quickly realized that I was out of my element. That was the first time I would ever step foot on a college campus, and felt like I didn't even belong.

I enrolled into four classes my first semester and was determined to challenge myself at getting better. Because I was still on house arrest, I was only allowed to go to school and back home. I quickly realized that as long as I was in school, that meant that I didn't have to be sitting around at home, bored out of my skull. I found refuge in the library and starting going after class regularly. When I needed help with math or writing a paper, I would go to the writing and math lab. I started attending my professor's office hours, that's how bad I didn't want to be home. I struggled profusely my first semester, but I knew that if I failed, I was going to be sent back to jail. When I would get a paper with an F on it, I would be scared to fail the class and have my judge be mad at me. I would make sure that I did everything I could to keep my grades up -- I was done with jail. The first semester finally came to an end, and I received a 3.79 GPA. I couldn't believe that all those A's were next to my name. I showed up to my next court date very happy to show the judge all my good progress.

She was so happy to hear how well I was doing that I got my house arrest terminated, but I was still on probation. That semester, I also finished my independent studies and was allowed to walk the stage and receive my high school diploma. I turned 18, and suddenly, things weren't looking so bad. I was done with high school and received honors in my first semester. It seemed like life was too good to be true.

# 8
## College Boy

*"Reality is wrong. Dreams are for real."*
*-Tupac Shakur*

I kept attending community college while taking care of my probation, and it was all going well. I couldn't help but notice that trouble was always around the corner and if I allowed myself to, I could end up right back in the hole again. While I was going to school and getting better, all my friends stayed the same, for the most part. I never stopped being around drugs or violence

-- I just chose to stop doing it myself. I started realizing that after my homework was done, I could continue to hang out with my friends and be out all day, so that's what I would do. I would leave the library around 2 p.m. with all my homework completed. I learned how to handle my business in the morning, so that I would be free to do whatever I wanted in the afternoon. At the time, I was still with my ex-girlfriend, and I enrolled her into community college as well. We would go to class together and get our homework done together. After two years of Alameda, I found out that I was eligible to graduate and was very happy. I still didn't know what being a college graduate meant -- after all, I only enrolled to get out of probation. It was time to start looking for a cap and gown and start thinking about transferring to a 4-year university. At first, I was just happy to be graduating, so I didn't really care about what school I transferred to.

I wanted to use that opportunity to really get out of the neighborhood and have a college experience, like I'd seen in the movies. I didn't want to go to any of the local schools, because that meant living at my mom's house. I applied to 4 universities and got denied to all of them but one: Cal State University Chico. At the time, I was very excited - I had gotten accepted into a university. I accepted my admission and started preparing to move out there. Me and my mom drove for three hours to attend orientation. After being there for a couple of hours and checking out their campus, I knew that Chico is where I wanted to be. I had found roommates and a place to live and had even chosen my classes. A week before I was supposed to start classes, I found out that I had been dropped from all my classes because I couldn't pay tuition in time. At that time, I was waiting for my financial aid to kick in, but because I didn't submit a paper in time, my classes got dropped. A couple of days before class started, I found out that I wasn't going to be going to Chico State anymore, so I had to move back home.

This was very devastating - I had finally left the neighborhood, where danger kept calling to me, only to have to go back to it. I felt like everything was going wrong - why would God stop me from going to a university? This was the only chance I had to get out and do something with myself. I didn't have a plan B, so I just fell flat on my face. I was depressed for a while - I didn't really know what life had to offer me anymore. Since I had already graduated community college, there was not a lot of options for me. My mom and I decided that it was best if I re-enrolled into community college and tried applying again to other schools the next semester. I knew that I had to work harder than ever to make sure that the next semester, I wouldn't be denied and forced to stay at home. That semester at Alameda, I took classes full time, determined to get my GPA even higher. That semester, I ended up receiving a 4.0 GPA and boosted my GPA higher. My counselor talked to me about applying to universities, instead of state colleges. I wasn't sure what to make of it, because I didn't think I was worthy enough to make it into a prestigious university.

I was scared to get rejected and scared to realize I wasn't good enough to make it. I finally decided to go through with it and applied to eight universities. When the results came back, I found out that I had gotten denied from two schools and been accepted to six universities. Wow, six programs wanted me to attend their school. I was two years removed from doing jail time, and now I was getting ready to attend a university. I was really trying to experience the world, and at that time, I felt like leaving my neighborhood was the best thing for me. I looked at all my acceptance letters and made my decision. There was a school that was five hours from my house, which meant that I would have to move out of my mom's place. I decided to attend the University of California, Santa

Barbara. I didn't know what the city or campus looked like - I didn't go on a campus tour. I simply chose that campus because it was the farthest one from my house.

Shortly afterwards, I started looking at places to live on Craigslist and found a spot. My friend Tiny called me when he found out I was going to Santa Barbara - he told me he didn't like where he was currently at and wanted a change. Tiny decided to transfer jobs and move with me to Santa Barbara. Me and Tiny found a two bedroom apartment on Craigslist, so I drove down to Santa Barbara to go see it and pay my down payment. When I first got to Santa Barbara, I instantly fell in love - it was sunny, you could feel the ocean breeze, and everyone was outside playing drinking games. I payed for our rent and down-payment and came back to the Bay Area to pack my bags.

My last couple of weeks in the Bay Area were bittersweet - I was sad that I was leaving my friends and family, but I was also excited to be starting a new chapter in my life. Me and my girlfriend decided that it was best to end things and not try doing the long distance relationship thing. My last night was very memorable - all my friends sent me off with weed and shots of Hennessy. In the morning, we left for Santa Barbara, and just like that, one chapter ended and another chapter began.

# 9
## *Daydreaming*

*"I'm going to continue to stand with the people that are being oppressed."*
*—Colin Kaepernick*

My mom dropped me off in Santa Barbara and turned around and went back home. Just like that, I was 20 years old and living on my own. I had my own place, and I had to cook for myself and take care of myself for the first time. As soon as I settled in, I went outside to try and make friends. I remember going around and trying to introduce myself to people, but I noticed they were nothing like me. At the time, I was dressing very ghetto, with saggy jeans and big shirts. It's understandable why the white kids weren't trying to talk to me. I was upset that I was struggling to make friends, so I would just stay in my apartment and smoke weed. My friend Tiny moved in a week later. That summer was going very badly, as I couldn't find anyone to hang out with. Santa Barbara is made up of a lot of rich white kids that I had nothing in common with. I would call my mom and tell her how much I hated living in this new environment. School didn't start for another two months, so I decided to go back home for the rest of the summer. I had a chance to be in the Bay Area again for a few more weeks before I really had to go back to school. I moved back to Santa Barbara two days before school started and began preparing for school. I started class a few days later, and it was really amazing.

The campus was so big, which made it easy for someone to get lost. I still needed to make friends and get invitations to parties. I decided to join a frat in order to make friends. The initiation process was crazy -- I didn't know much about frats, only the hazing and the stuff they would make people do. The first night, they had us wear suits and come to their house, where they initiated us. The rest of the process included hazing, stupid events, and a bunch of random stuff in between. I met a lot of great friends though the fraternity, people I will know for the rest of my life. We would party and drink everyday, and my grades reflected it. My first semester, I got placed on academic probation after failing all of my classes. I was forced to bring my GPA above a 2.0, or I would be kicked out of school. I was not going to allow the school system to wash me out. What was I going to tell my friends back home? That I didn't have what it took to succeed?

I had to remember why I was at school in the first place. I wasn't there to party, I was there to make sure I graduated from school. I had to reshape my mentality and get my GPA above a 2.0 if I wanted to stay in good standing. I ended up raising my grades and got off academic probation. I can honestly say the two years I spent in Santa Barbara were among the best years of my life. From showing up there at 20 years old, only having experienced San Leandro and Oakland, I was forced to grow on the fly. I was out of my comfort zone and had to excel in a different city. After two years in Santa Barbara, I was able to graduate and receive my bachelor's in Sociology. I was 22 years old with a bachelor's degree. In four short years, I was able to escape the judicial system and excel academically. To this day, I don't think that it was my freewill alone that allowed me to thrive. I think God placed me on this Earth to be an example of what happens when you commit to excellence.

I learned a lot of valuable things in school, but the most important thing that I gained was being able to navigate academia. I have met new people because of school, which has allowed me to open my mind up and see life differently. I don't think it was the actual material that I learned in class that was valuable, but it gave me the discipline needed to stay composed in life.

I literally went from being on probation to applying to graduate school in a matter of a few years. I'm currently attending San Francisco State University, where I'm pursuing my Master's degree in education. I'm on pace to graduate this June, in 2018. Me and my mother's relationship is a lot better now that I am older. I realize that she was the only person there, that was with me through it all. No matter how hard the situation was, she was there for the entire time. I have learned to appreciate my mom for being a warrior and never giving up on me. She showed me what a hard worker was and gave me my valuable work ethic. Me and my mom have a special bond -- she got to witness me at my lowest and highest points as a man.

My current goals are to keep going to school and receive my Phd from Harvard. I want to do great things in this world and inspire others to do the same. I want to be the education director at a juvenile hall and change the curriculum in those kinds of facilities. I believe that kids don't come out better than when they go into juvenile hall. With my story, I plan on helping others and pushing education forward. I think my story is a testament of resiliency and dedication. No matter if your back is against the wall, if you really want something, you can go get it. I'm currently still undocumented, without any legal status. I technically can't get a job, or even put my bachelors degree to use - luckily, my boss allows me to work without it. There are a lot of things that still bring me down emotionally. I still find myself crying sometimes because of how hard struggling can get. I try to put that all to the side and just remain positive. I am currently 23 years old, and this is my story. I want this book to remain relevant in ten years, as I feel people will always relate to my story. I don't know what the future has in store for me, but I am ready for anything life throws at me. I want everyone that reads this book to challenge themselves to be better.

Some tools that I would recommend are to think about your dreams and make a plan on how you will obtain them. Commit to yourself and don't be afraid to fail, that's part of the learning process. You will fall on your face at some point, but thats when you trust in yourself that everything you work for will pay off. Learn to love yourself, we are all beautiful and we're put on this place for a reason. And lastly, I believe that the kind of music you listen to reflects on your everyday life. Start listening to positive music and you will start to see a change. I recommend everyone to listen to *Friday Night Lights, and the Warm Up* by J. Cole. His music sends a positive message, even though he still had to go through the struggle to get to where he is at today.

If there was anything you ever dreamt about doing, go out into the world and achieve it. It takes a lot of patience and dedication, but I believe that it can be done. This being my first book, I didn't know what to expect as far as people actually reading through the entire piece. If you are still reading this, I would like to thank you, as this means a lot to me. A lot of these stories were buried in my head, so for me to write them down and publish them took a lot of courage. If my story can resonate with some of you, or make you want to follow your dreams, then this book was successful. My name is Manny Flores, and this is my story.

Made in the USA
Middletown, DE
13 September 2023

38482404R00046